YOUR FAVORITE STARS

FEATURING

SIMONE BILES

FACTS, QUIZZES, ACTIVITIES, AND MORE!

by Erin Falligant

CAPSTONE PRESS
a capstone imprint

This is an unauthorized biography.

Published by Capstone Press, an imprint of Capstone
1710 Roe Crest Drive, North Mankato, Minnesota 56003
capstonepub.com

Copyright © 2026 by Capstone. All rights reserved. No part of this publication may be reproduced in whole or in part, or stored in a retrieval system, or transmitted in any form or by any means, electronic, mechanical, photocopying, recording, or otherwise, without written permission of the publisher.

Library of Congress Cataloging-in-Publication Data
Names: Falligant, Erin, author.
Title: Featuring Simone Biles : facts, quizzes, activities, and more! / by Erin Falligant.
Description: North Mankato, Minnesota : Capstone Press, [2026] | Series: Your favorite stars | Audience: Ages 8-11 | Audience: Grades 4-6 | Summary: "How many gymnastics skills are named after Simone Biles? What animal is her good luck charm? Why was the 2024 Olympics considered Simone's redemption tour? Fans can read all about this and more in this collection of fun facts, fantastic photos, infographs, and more, featuring the gymnastics GOAT!"— Provided by publisher.
Identifiers: LCCN 2024059544 (print) | LCCN 2024059545 (ebook) | ISBN 9798875233173 (hardcover) | ISBN 9798875233128 (paperback) | ISBN 9798875233135 (pdf) | ISBN 9798875233142 (epub) | ISBN 9798875233159 (kindle edition)
Subjects: LCSH: Biles, Simone, 1997—Juvenile literature. | Women gymnasts—United States—Biography—Juvenile literature. | African American women athletes—United States—Biography—Juvenile literature. | African American women Olympic athletes—United States—Biography—Juvenile literature. | Women Olympic athletes—Mental health—Juvenile literature.
Classification: LCC GV460.2.B55 F35 2026 (print) | LCC GV460.2.B55 (ebook) | DDC 796.44092 [B]—dc23/eng/20241214
LC record available at https://lccn.loc.gov/2024059544
LC ebook record available at https://lccn.loc.gov/2024059545

Editorial Credits
Editor: Julie Gassman; Designer: Elyse White; Media Researcher: Rebekah Hunstenberger; Production Specialist: Tori Abraham

Image Credits
Alamy: Barry King, 35; Associated Press: Geert vanden Wijngaert, 42-43; Getty Images: Alex Wong, 31 (bottom right), Charley Gallay, 12, Elsa, 22, Emilee Chinn, 33, Emma McIntyre, 16, Ezra Shaw, 19, Harry How, 23, Jamie Squire, cover (middle), 6 (Victor Wembanyama), 11, 26, 40, Julian Finney, 45, Kristy Sparow, 36 (middle right), Laurence Griffiths, 18, 20, 37, 47, Michael Reaves, 6 (Jonathan Owens), 13, Naomi Baker, 24, 31 (middle), 41, Pascal Le Segretain, 5, 15, Patrick Smith, 7 (Simone Biles), 38, Ryan Pierse, 25, Sanja Baljkas, 7 (elephant), Unique Nicole, 32 (bottom right); Shutterstock: Alenini, 17 (bottom right), ANNA ZASIMOVA (rainbow chrome star), back cover and throughout, ArtHub02, 9 (pizza), Artorn Thongtukit, 7 (camel), derter (chrome sparkle), back cover and throughout, Doloves, 14 (umbrella), gillmar, 7 (polar bear), Jon Spalding, 17 (top right), Kseniia Khomyakova, 4, lilia_ahapova, 36 (heart), Magicleaf, 27, Mashaart (silver chrome star), back cover and throughout, Maxim Lysenko, 9 (Texas icon), Monica Polito, cover (gymnastics icon), Oleksandra Klestova (medal), cover, 5, Olena Go, 30 (medal), omravestudio, 14 (raindrops), Pavlo S, (colored curved stripes), cover, 28-29, Soifer, 34, Thx4Stock team, 44, Tuba Reza, 32 (heart chat icon), v_kulieva (blurry heart background), front and back cover and throughout, Zoya Zhuravliova, 39

Printed and bound in China. 6274

TABLE OF CONTENTS

**CHAPTER 1:
THE GOAT**.................................. 4

**CHAPTER 2:
FAMILY FIRST**........................... 12

**CHAPTER 3:
MAKING HISTORY**.................... 18

**CHAPTER 4:
OLYMPIC GOLD**........................ 24

**CHAPTER 5:
FASHION SENSE**....................... 32

**CHAPTER 6:
RISING UP** 40

CHAPTER 1

THE GOAT

SIMONE ARIANNE BILES is the most decorated U.S. gymnast in Olympic history. She has earned more medals than any other gymnast on the U.S. team! Fans and other athletes consider her the GOAT, the **Greatest of All Time**. But she's also known for her smile, her style, her team spirit, and her strength in overcoming challenges.

STAR SCOOP!

Simone has *five* gymnastics skills named after her: two on vault, two on floor, and one on beam. She was the first woman to ever perform them in international competitions.

SHE CAN JUMP!

At the 2024 Olympic trials, Simone's head got 12 feet (3.6 meters) above the mat during her floor routine. That means she could jump over . . .

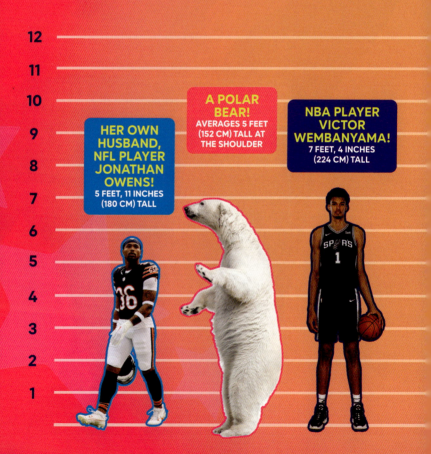

HER OWN HUSBAND, NFL PLAYER JONATHAN OWENS!
5 FEET, 11 INCHES (180 CM) TALL

A POLAR BEAR!
AVERAGES 5 FEET (152 CM) TALL AT THE SHOULDER

NBA PLAYER VICTOR WEMBANYAMA!
7 FEET, 4 INCHES (224 CM) TALL

A CAMEL! AVERAGES 7 FEET (213 CM) TALL AT THE HUMP

AN ASIAN ELEPHANT! AVERAGES 9 FEET (274 CM) TALL AT THE SHOULDER

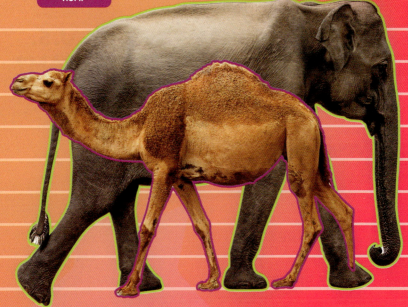

SMALL BUT MIGHTY

At four feet eight inches (142 centimeters) tall, Simone was the shortest U.S. athlete at the 2024 Olympics. Simone tires of people asking about her height. She said, "I love my body because it helps with gymnastics and it teaches the other girls to love their bodies as well."

When it comes to gymnastics, being short can definitely be a good thing! Shorter gymnasts can rotate their bodies quickly and may stick their landings more easily.

HOW TALL WAS THE 2024 U.S. WOMEN'S GYMNASTICS TEAM?

- **SIMONE BILES:** 4'8" (142 CM)
- **JORDAN CHILES:** 4'11" (150 CM)
- **SUNI LEE:** 5'0" (152 CM)
- **JADE CAREY:** 5'2" (157 CM)
- **HEZLY RIVERA:** DOES NOT SHARE HER HEIGHT

GET TO KNOW SIMONE!

Is each statement **TRUE OR FALSE**?

1. Simone was born in Texas.
2. She has a little sister.
3. She was homeschooled in elementary school.
4. Her favorite food is pizza.
5. Her least favorite food is coconut.
6. Simone is afraid of bulldogs.
7. Her favorite gymnastics event is floor.
8. Her least favorite event is beam.

ANSWERS:

1. FALSE. She lives in Texas but was born in Columbus, Ohio, on March 14, 1997.

2. TRUE. Her sister, Adria, is 2 years younger, and she used to be a gymnast too.

3. FALSE. Simone wasn't homeschooled until high school, when she chose to make more time for gymnastics.

4. TRUE. It's tradition for her to eat pepperoni pizza after a competition, and she loves stuffed crust.

5. TRUE. She just doesn't like the taste!

6. **FALSE.** In fact, she is the proud fur mama of two French bulldogs, Lilo and Rambo, and co-parent to her husband's English bulldog, Zeus.

7. **TRUE.** She loves floor because she gets to show off her personality.

8. **FALSE.** It's bars. But she says, "I'm learning to love it and I'm getting better at it."

STAR SCOOP!

Simone says that if she weren't a gymnast, she would be a nurse for babies in the intensive care unit. She loves babies!

CHAPTER **2**

FAMILY FIRST

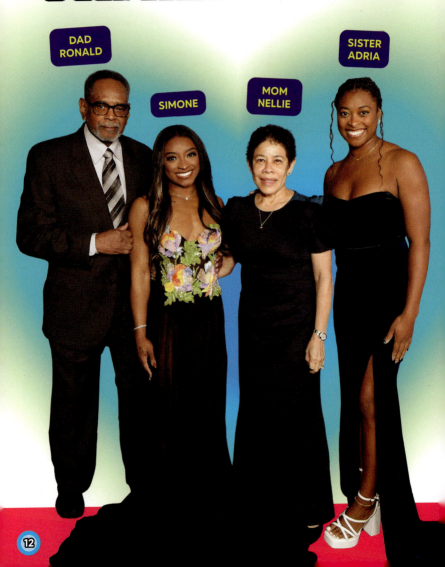

IN THE BEGINNING

Simone's grandparents, **Ronald and Nellie Biles**, adopted her and her little sister, **Adria**, when Simone was only 6. Their biological mom suffered from substance abuse and couldn't take care of them. Simone calls her grandparents "Mom" and "Dad" and says her family means the world to her. That family now includes her husband, pro football player **Jonathan Owens**, and their beloved dogs.

STAR SCOOP!

Simone got her first dog by winning a bet. Her dad said if she did well in a tournament, he would buy her a dog. She placed first on floor and second all-around—and got a German shepherd!

HER BIGGEST FANS

Simone gives her parents credit for her success. They homeschooled her so she could focus on gymnastics, and they even opened a gymnastics center in Texas where she could train! Simone's parents have attended every big competition, except for the **2020 Olympics** due to the pandemic. Simone looks for them in the stands and says that seeing them calms her down.

STAR SCOOP!

Simone owes her career to bad weather! When she was 6, her day care planned a field trip to a ranch. When it got rained out, they went to a gymnastics center instead. And the rest is history . . .

Husband Jonathan Owens joined Simone's parents Nellie and Ronald as Simone's biggest fans at the 2024 Olympics.

GOOD LUCK CHARMS

Simone's mom, Nellie, thinks it is funny that people call Simone the GOAT. To Nellie, Simone is her "**Little Turtle**." She gave her the nickname years ago to remind her to take her time and be herself. Now turtles are Simone's good luck charm! Her mom gives her turtle figurines before important competitions. They have sayings on them like "Go at your own pace" and "One step at a time."

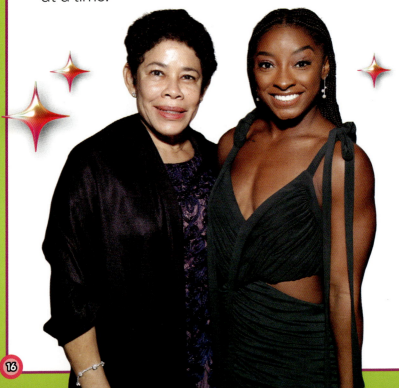

PAINT A TURTLE!

MAKE A GOOD LUCK TURTLE OF YOUR OWN! HERE'S HOW:

1. Find a smooth rock outside, or buy one at a craft store.

2. Wash and dry the rock.

3. Paint the rock with acrylic paint. Let the paint dry.

4. Use a paint marker or permanent marker to add a quote. Try one of these:

   Slow and steady wins the race!

   Slow progress is still progress!

   Keep moving forward!

   Take it one step at a time!

CHAPTER 3
MAKING HISTORY

Simone's favorite school subject was history. Ever since then, she's been making history! She constantly pushes herself to try new things. Because of her courage and creativity, she has forever changed the sport of gymnastics.

WHY SHE'S THE GOAT

- **30 WORLD MEDALS—THE MOST IN GYMNASTICS HISTORY**

- **23 WORLD GOLD MEDALS—THE MOST IN GYMNASTICS HISTORY**

- **FIRST WOMAN TO WIN 6 WORLD ALL-AROUND TITLES**

- **FIRST WOMAN TO WIN 4 WORLD BALANCE BEAM TITLES**

- **FIRST WOMAN TO WIN 6 WORLD FLOOR EXERCISE TITLES**

- **MOST DECORATED GYMNAST OF ALL TIME**

SIMONE'S MILESTONES

2013 — Becomes the first Black woman to win the all-around gymnastics title at the World Championships.

Has a gymnastics skill named after her for the first time! The Biles I on floor exercise is a double layout with a half-twist in the second flip.

2015 — Becomes the first female gymnast to win the all-around title at World Championships three years in a row.

2016 — Is the first female U.S. gymnast to win four gold medals at a single Olympic Games since 1974.

2018 — Becomes the first U.S. gymnast to medal in every event at a single World Championships.

Gets a vault skill named after her for the first time! The Biles I on vault is a half-twist onto the vaulting table and a double twisting somersault off.

2019

Gets a second floor move named after her. The Biles II on floor exercise is a triple-double with two flips and three twists.

Has a beam skill named after her for the first time! The Biles on balance beam is a double-double dismount with two twists and two flips.

2021

Becomes the first gymnast to land the Yurchenko double pike on vault at the U.S. Classic.

2023

Earns her 34th medal across the World Championships and Olympics, making her the most decorated gymnast ever.

Does the Yurchenko double pike on vault for the first time in an international competition. Now it's known as the Biles II on vault!

2024

Earns four medals at the 2024 Summer Olympics, bringing her total count to 11—more than any other U.S. gymnast has won in Olympic history.

At age 27, becomes the oldest U.S. female gymnast to win Olympic gold.

STAR SCOOP!

Simone says she's still scared every time she does the **Yurchenko double pike** on vault. It's a very difficult and dangerous move!

WHAT'S AGE GOT TO DO WITH IT?

During the 2024 Paris Olympics, Simone got a lot of attention for something other than her skills—her age! At 27, she was USA Gymnastics' oldest team member. And she was the oldest American woman to compete in gymnastics since the 1952 Olympics, more than 70 years earlier.

Gymnastics is a sport where teenagers often rack up the medals. In fact, the last three all-around Olympic titles before Paris were all won by teenagers, including Biles herself in 2016.

STAR SCOOP!

Aly Raisman, Simone's former teammate, held the record for oldest U.S. female gymnast to win gold before Simone. Aly was 22 when she earned the title at the 2016 Summer Olympics.

CHAPTER 4
OLYMPIC GOLD

Simone has competed—and medaled—in three Olympics Games: Rio de Janeiro in 2016, Tokyo in 2020, and Paris in 2024. After medaling in the Games, it's a tradition for Simone and her teammates to give themselves a nickname.

2024's Golden Girls

STAR SCOOP!

The 2016 team called themselves the "**Final Five**" for two reasons. They were the last team coached by **Marta Karolyi**, and only *four* women would be allowed on the team at the 2020 Olympics.

They were the "Final Five" in 2016, the "Fighting Four" in 2020, and the "Golden Girls" in 2024—because they were some of the oldest female gymnasts to compete on Team USA!

THE TWISTIES

At the 2020 Olympics, Simone planned to perform the Amanar vault, which no female athlete had ever done. But instead of doing two and a half twists off the vaulting table, she got confused and did only one and a half.

Simone had "**the twisties**," a mental block that can be dangerous. When gymnasts lose their place in the air, they can fall and get seriously hurt. Simone withdrew from the rest of the events except beam, and she thought she might never compete again. But she did!

Simone's twisties led to a stumbled landing on vault the day before she withdrew from the competition.

THE 2020 SUMMER OLYMPICS

The games were actually held in 2021 because of the pandemic.

Athletes were tested for COVID-19 every day.

No fans were allowed in the stands.

Gymnasts were required to wear masks during practice.

Athletes were allowed to go only from the hotel to the gym and back again.

PARIS 2024

Simone competed in the 2024 Olympics in Paris. How much do you know about those Olympics? Take this quiz to find out!

1. Which gymnast was *not* a teammate of Simone's in 2024?

   A. Jordan Chiles
   B. Jade Carey
   C. Gabby Douglas

2. Who was Simone's toughest competitor in Paris?

   A. Rebeca Andrade of Brazil
   B. Suni Lee of the U.S.
   C. Zhang Qingying of China

3. What injury was Simone dealing with?

　　A. A sprained ankle
　　B. A calf injury
　　C. A broken toe

4. Which Taylor Swift song did Simone perform to at the start of her floor routine?

　　A. ". . . Ready for It?"
　　B. "Shake It Off"
　　C. "You Need to Calm Down"

5. Simone and her teammates called the Games their "_____ Tour."

　　A. Revolution
　　B. Domination
　　C. Redemption

1. C, 2. A, 3. B, 4. A, 5. C

MEDAL COUNT

SIMONE'S OLYMPIC MEDALS

	GOLD	SILVER	BRONZE
7	2024 Team		
6	2024 All-Around		
5	2024 Vault		
4	2016 Team		
3	2016 All-Around		
2	2016 Vault	2024 Floor	2020 Beam
1	2016 Floor	2020 Team	2016 Beam

STAR SCOOP!

Simone received a medal of a *different* kind on July 7, 2022. President Biden awarded her the Presidential Medal of Freedom for her contributions to her sport.

CHAPTER **5**

FASHION SENSE

Simone has fun with fashion both in and out of the gym. She has partnered with fitness brands **Nike** and **Athleta**, and even launched her own line of Athleta activewear in 2020. But she also loves to put the leotards away, get her nails done, and dress up. She says, "It's good to have that balance—to not just always be thinking about the gym."

Simone wore a rhinestone goat on her leotard at a competition in 2021.

STAR SCOOP!

Simone wore a diamond GOAT necklace after winning all-around gold at the 2024 Olympics! People call her the Greatest of All Time, but she says she's just "Simone Biles from Spring, Texas, that loves to flip."

TEN MAGAZINE COVERS STARRING SIMONE

1. *EBONY*
2. *ESSENCE*
3. *GLAMOUR*
4. *NEW YORK MAGAZINE*
5. *PEOPLE*
6. *SPORTS ILLUSTRATED*
7. *TEEN VOGUE*
8. *TIME*
9. *VANITY FAIR*
10. *VOGUE*

Simone was the focus of *Rising*, a two part documentary series on Netflix.

ONSCREEN AND IN THE SPOTLIGHT

Photoshoots used to terrify Simone. Now she has fun with them and lets her personality shine through. She has also been interviewed on many television shows and in documentaries. When Simone talks about her journey as an athlete and the challenges she has faced, people listen. She has shared her story with audiences all around the world!

ALL ABOUT HAIR

Gymnastics hairdos have gone from basic buns and ponytails to braids with glitter. Athletes can be more creative than ever before. But the textured hair of Black athletes hasn't always been accepted.

Simone fights back against negative comments online. In a social media post, she wrote, "Next time you wanna comment on a black girl's hair. **JUST DON'T**." She has learned to love her hair and the styles she can create.

STAR SCOOP!

Gymnasts don't have a professional hairstylist at the Olympics. Simone says teammate Jordan Chiles was the official "hair braider" for the 2024 Olympic team.

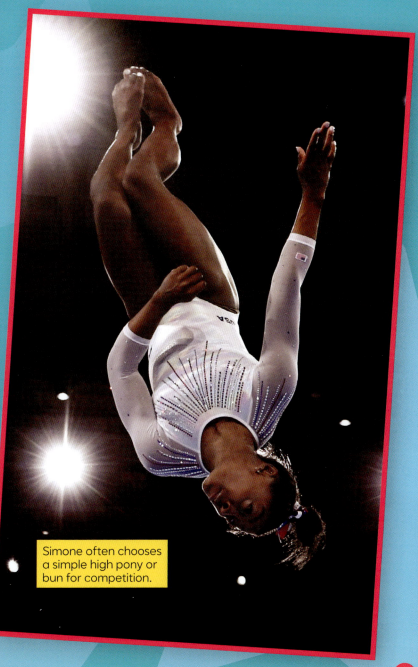

Simone often chooses a simple high pony or bun for competition.

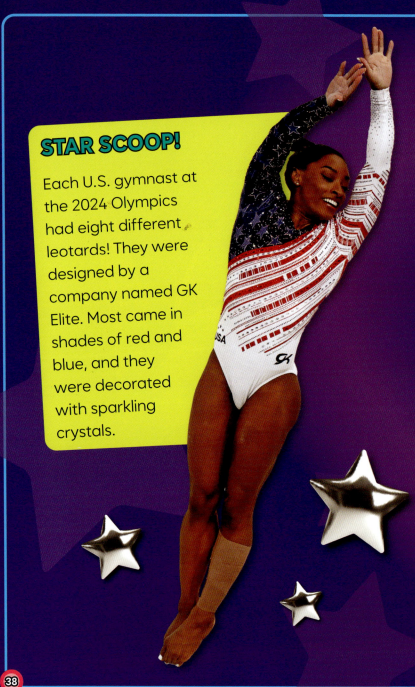

STAR SCOOP!

Each U.S. gymnast at the 2024 Olympics had eight different leotards! They were designed by a company named GK Elite. Most came in shades of red and blue, and they were decorated with sparkling crystals.

DESIGN A LEO

The leotard that Simone wore for the all-around final was inspired by Wonder Woman's armor. (See it at left!) The stars and crystal lines on the sleeves represent the American flag! Can you design a leotard that represents your strengths and interests? Trace this leo, and decorate it in your own unique way.

CHAPTER 6
RISING UP

Simone's childhood wasn't easy. She and her little sister were in foster care before going to live with their grandparents. Simone says she'll never forget where she came from and how it shaped her as a person. "Whenever you're in foster care, and you come out of it, the odds are against you," she says. But that made her fight harder to reach her goals.

"If somebody told me I couldn't do something, it was up to me to prove I could."

STAR SCOOP!

Simone wants to help other kids in foster care. She started the Simone Biles Legacy Scholarship Fund to help foster children attend college.

OTHER CHALLENGES SIMONE OVERCAME

- Being diagnosed with ADHD

- *Not* making the U.S. women's junior national team in 2011 (she missed it by one spot!)

- Being the only Black girl on the team sometimes—and not having enough role models

- Trying to train during the pandemic

- Speaking out against abuse at the Dr. Larry Nassar trial

STAR SCOOP!

When Simone won the all-around at the 2023 World Championships, the second and third place winners were also Black gymnasts. Simone called it "**Black girl magic**" and hopes it inspired young Black girls to dream big.

The 2023 World Championships all-around medalists included (from left to right) Brazil's Rebeca Andrade, and U.S. gymnasts Simone Biles and Shilese Jones.

PUTTING MENTAL HEALTH FIRST

After Simone got the twisties in 2020, she took time off to get counseling. She went back to basic skills at the gym, like flips on the trampoline. She didn't want other gymnasts to see how scared she was, but it helped her to spend time with them. "I wanted to quit like five hundred thousand times," she says, "and I would have if it weren't for my people." She shares her story so that other young athletes know it's okay to put their mental health first.

STAR SCOOP!

Now when Simone feels stressed at competitions, she practices visualization. She takes deep breaths and pictures herself at her happy place—the beach! Or she wears the color red to feel strong and powerful.

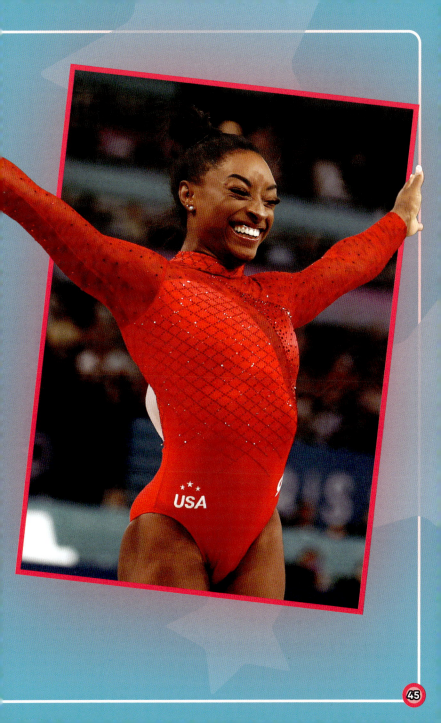

SIMONE SAYS . . .

"I'm not the next Usain Bolt or Michael Phelps. I'm the first Simone Biles."

"I do not have it all together, but I can be there with you guys every step of the way while we figure this out together."

"You can be short or tall, and your body type doesn't matter because you can do anything."

STAR SCOOP!

Simone got a tattoo in 2021 that reads "And still I rise," a line from a Maya Angelou poem. "After all of the traumas and the downfalls," Simone says, "I've always risen."

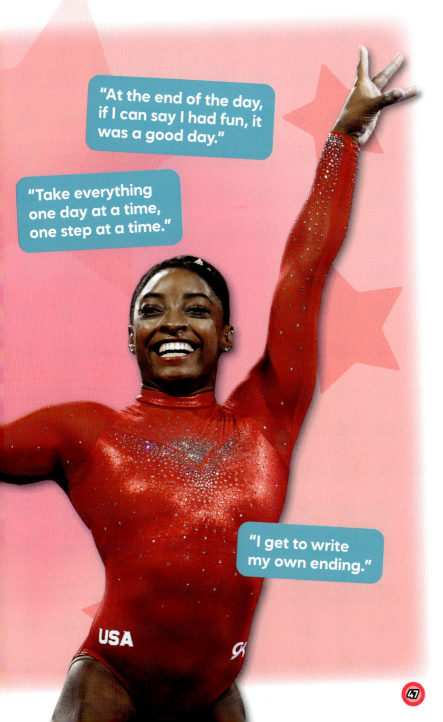

ABOUT THE AUTHOR

Erin Falligant has written more than 50 books for children. An experienced author with a versatile voice, she writes fiction based on beloved toy and animation properties such as American Girl, Disney, Minecraft, and Pokémon. Her Joss series for American Girl, written about a young surfer with hearing loss, earned a 2020 Moonbeam Gold Medal Award. To learn more about Erin and her books, visit www.erinfalligant.com

READ MORE ABOUT YOUR FAVORITE STARS

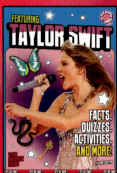